CHEWING WATER

Other Poetry Books By Nelson Ball

Two Poems (press-press-pull/alabastine press, 2015
This Close To Being A Tree (Monk Press, 2015)
Thirty Poems (Rubblestone Press, 2015)
Small Waterways (Apt. 9 Press, 2015)
Farmer's Dell Plaza (press-press-pull/alabastine press, 2015
All And Everything (Laurel Reed Books, 2015)
Some Mornings (Mansfield Press, 2014)
You Must Look Hard To See What's There (press-press-pull, 2014)
Three-Letter Words (2nd edition, press-press-pull, 2014)
A Rattle Of Spring Frogs (Hamilton Arts & Letters, 2014, online)
Minutiae (Apt. 9 Press, 2014)
A Gathering (new edition, BookThug, 2014)
Orphans (Rubblestone Press, 2012)
The Continuous Present (Proper Tales Press, 2012)
In This Thin Rain (Mansfield Press, 2012)
Nine Poems (Rubblestone Press, 2011)
Three-Letter Words (Laurel Reed Books, 2006)
At The Edge Of The Frog Pond (The Mercury Press, 2004)
With Held (Laurel Reed Books, 2004)
Scrub Cedar (above/ground press, 2003)
A Gathering (Rubblestone Press, 2003)
Almost Spring (The Mercury Press, 1999)
Visitation (Rubblestone Press, 1998)
To Share That Yellow (fingerprinting inkoperated, 1998)
The Concrete Air (The Mercury Press, 1996)
Round Table (Letters, 1996)
Small Gardens (fingerprinting inkoperated, 1996)
Bird Tracks On Hard Snow (ECW Press, 1994)
Fifteen Poems (MindWare, 1994)
Sightings (Curvd H&z, 1992)
With Issa: Poems 1964-1971 (ECW Press, 1991)
Force Movements (2nd edition, Curvd H&z, 1990)
Round Stone (Weed/Flower Press, 1971)
Points Of Attention (Weed/Flower Press, 1971)
The Pre-Linguistic Heights (Coach House Press, 1970)
Water-Pipes And Moonlight (Weed/Flower Press, 1969)
Force Movements (Ganglia Press, 1969)
Sparrows (Weed/Flower Press, 1968)
Beaufort's Scale (Weed/Flower Press, 1967)
Room Of Clocks (Weed/Flower Press, 1965)

Books Edited

Konfessions Of An Elizabethan Fan Dancer by bpNichol (Coach House Books, 2004)
Frank Harrington's Kristmiss Book (The Mercury Press, 1993)

CHEWING WATER

NELSON BALL

Mansfield Press

a stuart ross book

Library and Archives Canada Cataloguing in Publication

Ball, Nelson, 1942-, author
Chewing water / Nelson Ball.

Poems.
ISBN 978-1-77126-105-0 (paperback)

I. Title.

PS8503.A59C44 2016 C811'.54 C2016-901474-6

Editor for the press: Stuart Ross
Cover design: Denis De Klerck
Cover image: Shutterstock
Typesetting: Stuart Ross
Author photo: Laurie Siblock

The publication of *Chewing Water* has been generously supported by the Canada Council for the Arts and the Ontario Arts Council.

Canada Council for the Arts
Conseil des Arts du Canada

ONTARIO ARTS COUNCIL
CONSEIL DES ARTS DE L'ONTARIO
an Ontario government agency
un organisme du gouvernement de l'Ontario

Mansfield Press Inc.
25 Mansfield Avenue, Toronto, Ontario, Canada M6J 2A9
Publisher: Denis De Klerck
www.mansfieldpress.net

To my wonderful friend Catherine Stevenson

&

In memory of my soulmate, Barbara Caruso

Contents

Becky Taylor / 9
All And Everything / 10
Spider / 11
Trying To See What's There / 12
Catherine Visits / 13
The Quest For Knowledge / 14
This Close To Being A Tree / 15
Sunday Morning In Southwestern Ontario / 16
Orderliness / 17
The Meaning Of Death / 18
The Meaning Of Life / 19
Love Bird / 20
I Chased Birds / 21
Juniper's / 22
Early Fall / 23
Fall / 24
Affiliations And Afflictions / 26
Barbara And Me / 28
Cheese Sticks / 29
Ant / 30
My Neighbour / 31
Local Wildlife / 32
Recycling / 33
Regifting: December 22, 2014 / 34
Short Takes / 35
Taylor Trail, Varna, Ontario / 39
A Frog Pond's Lover's / 40
My Friend Catherine / 41
Barbara / 42
Canada / 43
Citizenship / 44
Farmer's Dell Plaza / 45
For / 46

Crow Call / 47
Ducks / 48
In A Field Near Paris, Ontario / 49
My Tinnitus Crickets / 50
Preference / 51
At The Restaurant / 52
Bird / 53
Fortuitous / 54
The Dead / 55
In Sunlight / 56
Lake Huron Shoreline, Revised / 57
Light / 58
Friends And Flies / 59
After The Visitors Stop Coming / 60
Living With Severe Emphysema / 61
Perception / 62
September 5, 2014 / 63
She Would Have Named Them Nubbies / 64
Windy Night / 65
Yacht / 66
Words / 67
Under The Bark / 68
Privet / 69
In Spring / 70
On A Hilltop, Near Drumbo / 71
Tamarack / 72
Northville Plaza / 73
Strange / 74
"That was $150 not well spent" / 75
Signs: May / 76
Rhyme / 77
A Speeding Squirrel's / 78
Winter Will Come / 79
Ampersand / 80
To Kate Belair / 81

Windy / 82
This Day / 83
More Than A Fashion Statement / 84
A King Kong Of A Weed / 85
Private Conversations / 86
July 3, 2014—Three Performances / 87
It's Spring! / 88
Chewing Water / 89
Retinal Retention / 90
Barbara Dying / 91
Spring / 92
Whereness / 93
Birthdays / 94
A Chipmunk Mystery / 95
In My Old Age / 96
Fishing / 97
My Friend / 98
Bucolic / 99
Yikes! / 100
Woodlots, Old Cemeteries, Lanes / 101
Campbell Trail, Ayr, Ontario / 102
April And May / 103
After Major Surgery / 104
Notes / 107
Acknowledgements / 117

Becky Taylor

When I was five
Becky Taylor was my best friend.

Her dad was a policeman.
I didn't know what a policeman did.

His car had words and numbers on it.
He went away in the morning and came home for supper.

Becky and I rode our tricycles
and her mother

fed us cookies.
What a fine life that was!

All And Everything

George Ivanovitch Gurdjieff, 1872?–1949

Rain
patters on the window pane

a
sound

alone
connecting

all
and everything

Spider

A long-legged spider
in a ceiling corner

for weeks
motionless

until
last evening

it lifted
each leg

slowly
deliberately

high
stepping

then
stillness—

a slow
dance

this
spider's life

Trying To See What's There

I'm
troubled by

how
much

I didn't see
before

that
now I see

Catherine Visits

For Catherine Stevenson

Catherine
likes to visit this place

where I live
mostly in silence

she says
it is peaceful

compared to life
with her students

and her children
here she will

speak words
onto the still air

where
they breathe

and we
look at them

The Quest For Knowledge

For Heather Smith, and Isaiah

Heather's
the young woman who cleans my home.

We talk. That's more urgent
than housecleaning.

She studied history of religion
and English in university. She observes things

including Isaiah her three-year-old
who also observes things

and repeatedly
asks "Why?"

This Close To Being A Tree

On the toe cap
of my grey running shoe

sat a small grey object
that looked like a tree frog

but was in fact
a tiny piece of bark

I don't know how
it got there, but

it raises the question
am I so close

to being
a tree?

Sunday Morning In Southwestern Ontario

A man
goes to church

or
spends

all
morning

washing
his truck

Orderliness

With my sisters Mary and Liz in 2013
at our mother's childhood home

The Mossop home
on Bronson Line

in farmland
south of Bayfield

vacant
for many years

drapes in tatters
floor boards rotted

front door open
roof sagging

not yet collapsed
that's in the offing

Mary says a need of order
causes the farmer

to mow
the lawn.

The Meaning Of Death

It's
the
end

of
morning
coffee

The Meaning Of Life

For Jackie, who says

"It
is

what

it
is"

daubs
of
snow

on
dark
soil

are

daubs
of
snow

on
dark
soil

Love Bird

He hit the kitchen window
like a shotgun blast

left an explosion of small feathers
floating in air

rested briefly
on a nearby branch

before resuming
the dangerous pursuit.

I Chased Birds

I chased birds
with a salt shaker
when I was five

after my uncle told me
if I put salt on a bird's tail
I could catch it.

I never got salt
onto a bird's tail.
What a chump!

Juniper's

shadows
jiggle

on the steps
beside me

bringing
to light

an unfelt
breeze

Early Fall

Cornstalks
yellow

leaves
skitter

daylight
lessens

air
cools

sounds
sharpen

Fall

Autumn
asserts a coolness

at the edges
of August days

•

On the road—
caterpillars

rattling
leaves

pop
cans

•

On the pond—
fallen

leaves
set sail

•

In the forest's
silence

falling
leaves

tick
into place

•

Beside the pond
thump-thump

thump
thump

landing
walnuts

•

While a corn harvester
fills a grain truck

blocking
Blue Lake Road

I
wait

Affiliations And Afflictions

Catherine and her friend came to visit
on a winter afternoon.

They were bundled, and in the kerfuffle
of finding places for hats and scarves

and coats and boots, Catherine placed her purse
on my summer walking shoes.

We settled in to serious talk—Catherine's project
for a kids' summer camp at Wilfrid Laurier University,

my poet friend who's writing twelve books,
my stalled book of selected poems for Laurier.

When time to leave, Catherine couldn't find her purse.
Her friend pointed and, as Catherine picked it up, said

"Now you've put girl cooties on Nelson's shoes."
I wasn't sure I'd heard right.

That's what she said. She seems an unlikely comic,
and this so out of context amongst adults.

A friend remembers "girl cooties" as playground talk—
if a girl touched you, you got "girl cooties".

When I was young, cooties didn't have gender affiliation.
They were simply cooties. My sister says the same.

Another friend wrote "CV" on her hand
to vaccinate against them.

Barbara And Me

In memory of Barbara Caruso;
dedicated to Allison and Michael Casteels

Barbara was little and cute, as tall
as my shoulder. I am tall and sober.

She was the most serious and focused person
I have ever known. Almost one-track.

But she could be playful, too. Standing
in front of me, she

would snuggle her nose
into my shirt pocket.

Cheese Sticks

Barbara and I indulged,
occasionally, in junk food.

I was underweight
and Barbara was not overweight.

We liked Humpty Dumpty Cheese Sticks
although Barbara had reservations—

"They're filled with air" she noted, asking
"Where did that air come from,

where
has it been?"

She would not eat Aero bars
Coffee Crisp was okay

Dairy Milk
was the best.

Ant

I'm
a weakling

compared
to this ant carrying

a dead winged insect
four times

its
size

My Neighbour

For Jackie Morris

On most days she
bubbles with happiness, but

she came today
with tales of woe:

she fell off her bike
scraped an ankle, bruised her bum

she petted a dog
it bit her

a spider bit her foot
spreading purple across the skin

she went to Urgent Care
at the Willett Hospital

found it filled
with uncovered coughs

returned home
to her bed and sleep

Local Wildlife

We've driven out the bears
from most southern Ontario

killed the wolves
and rattlesnakes

we are left with chipmunks
lots of them, everywhere

up your pant leg
in your hair

raccoons
skunks

foxes
preying on chickens

a
coyote

eating
apples

Recycling

Dogs
eat

dog
poop

•

Hogs
eat
poop

in the mix of their feed:
some seeds

better digested
second time through

•

People
eat
poop

it's called fecal
transplant
therapy

treatment
for
C. difficile

Regifting: December 22, 2014

For Brian David Johnston and for Catherine Stevenson and her boys

For Christmas a friend gave me
an oversize eraser for "BIG MISTAKES"

and six miniature recycling bins
the size of coffee cups.

"What am I supposed to do with these bins?"
"Put your pencils in them."

A few days later Catherine brought her boys to visit. Aha!
The older boy looked puzzled on receiving the eraser.

His mother said it doesn't mean you make big mistakes,
but it gives you permission to do so.

He flexed the eraser to show his mother how
the shapes of the letters change. A visual poet in the making!

The younger boy went wild with the bins—
they were racing cars, their lids flapped and rattled,

he stacked them like blocks—
knocked over the stacks.

Catherine said if I'd spent $100
they would not have had more fun.

Short Takes

1

It's safe
to walk backwards

along
the hall

now
I live alone

2

A chipmunk
with the disadvantages of short legs

and an upraised tail
producing wind resistance

can nonetheless run
very fast

3

Standing
still

is
as close

as I
will ever be

to being
a tree

4

Life's
challenge:

avoid
a Void

5: Willow

Will
ill

•

ill
owl

•

ill
willow

•

Lil
low

6: Contradictory

Fluffy
white clouds

look
like

torn
and worried

cotton
batting

7: Church Sign

"God has thought
about you today"

Okay
so long as God wasn't watching

8: Church Sign

"God has thought
about you today"

And...?
What did God think?

9

An owl in
howling
wind

or
bowling

10: Birthday Parties

Why do we
celebrate

the passing of time
when life is

so
short?

Taylor Trail, Varna, Ontario

Inside
the pine plantation

a thickness
of dead branches and twigs

bed
of fallen needles

overhead
a green canopy

filters
light

a profound
silence

distance
viewed

along
a narrow path

A Frog Pond's Lover's

a
frog

or
another
frog

My Friend Catherine

For Catherine Stevenson, and in memory of Barbara

My friend Catherine is here today
in Barbara's second-floor studio

taking photographs for her documentary.
I hear above me the muted sound

of her feet, as she moves
room to room, back and forth

a sound just like Barbara's soft steps—
the lightness, the gentle rhythm.

This is comforting, evoking
a vivid memory of Barbara's presence

and it is evidence of this woman
who is not my lover, although I love her

but is my wonderful friend
who by her presence

leads me away
from enormous grief.

Barbara

A Remembrance

Inked
from holding *The Globe and Mail*

your thumb left its print
on the toilet seat

where it
remained

evoking
your warmth

Canada

For Ted Rushton

William Hawkins
remains in Ottawa, that cold city

where he writes poems about Tallahassee.
I remain in southwestern Ontario, where

occasionally it's as cold as Ottawa,
and where I puzzle about Arizona,

in its great distance
from our cold and snow.

It's irrational that we stay put.
My friend Catherine gives a reason:

our wild animals in this cool climate
don't want to eat us, except bears

who mostly hide from us in the forest.
In South Carolina, alligators

roam the streets and lawns
and one has to be nice to them.

Citizenship

Two days prior
to Canada Day

I'm reading
a Louise Penny novel

while hearing
bang-bang-bang

fireworks nearby.
This is what we do in southwestern Ontario—

set fire to things
that go bang.

Farmer's Dell Plaza

Barber shop
pizza shop

jeweller
insurance agent

chiropractor
laundromat

orthotist
acupuncturist

massage
therapist

convenience
store

a dealer
in cards, comics and collectables

commerce
conducted amid

exhaust
fumes—

no small valley
no farmer

For

A word possessing visual stability
in the formation of its letters

least secure is "o"
which is slippery

could go anywhere
but is locked in

the "r" is precarious
the overhang of a cliff

but the arms of the "F"
exert gravitational tension

pulling on the "r"
holding it in place.

Crow Call

For Patrick and Anita Campbell

Patrick
bought a crow call

he
knows why

I
don't

Anita
wonders

are the crows
confused

asking
each other

"What
is this guy

trying
to say?"

Ducks

Spring
rains

flood
fields—

every
farm

a
pond

In A Field Near Paris, Ontario

A willow
billows

wands
swaying in a breeze

quivering
wavering

like an overgrown
relocated

lumbering
muskox

My Tinnitus Crickets

There's a field of crickets
inside my head

a plentitude of friends
who sleep when I do

and greet me
every morning.

Preference

Four days remain
to file

my quarterly
GST/HST Tax Return

instead
I write this poem

At The Restaurant

For Catherine Stevenson

Owen
on the floor

pounces
like a cat

tries
to catch a fly that's

biting
his mother's ankle

Bird

My car passes over
a small bird

standing alert
at the centre of the road

it didn't move
is uninjured

seems
unperturbed

just young
pre-school

Fortuitous

A barn
on German School Road

has a hole
through the roof

for pigeons
and swallows

The Dead

weight
of

a
dead
worm

exceeds
the strength of two ants

struggling
at
each
end

to
move
it

In Sunlight

Fresh snow
covers the frozen pond

and surrounding ground
with a whiteness

except under the varnished picnic table
where reflected light

colours the snow
yellow

Lake Huron Shoreline, Revised

The water has retreated
leaving stones in hard mud

small waterways
between stones

soft mud engraved in long trails
of underwater snails

minnows
tadpoles

nearby cedars
not yet tall

Light

A dark
night

easy
rain

glistens
in pools

a car
approaches and passes

roadway
brightens

then
darkness

car's
light

gone
with the car

Friends And Flies

For Catherine and Clayton and Nick

In the kitchen at Waterford
while Catherine and Clayton

prepared and cooked tomato sauce
a fat fly hovered, intruding.

"It's a 30-day fly" said Clayton. "They live for 31"
he added on seeing my puzzled look.

I've written poems about flies, ignorant
of their life spans, so I read up on it.

In the tropics, they live faster
for two to three weeks.

In Thunder Bay, where Nick Drumbolis lives
they move slowly and live longer in the cold air.

Houseflies evolved in the Middle East
65 million years ago

and much later
accompanied human migration.

Like us, they
are everywhere.

After The Visitors Stop Coming

Ball's Cemetery, Hullett Township, Huron County

Beneath memorial stones
covered over

with lichen,
bird poop, and grasses

the dead
rest

Living With Severe Emphysema

For Jackie and Catherine

Young
friends

hug
me

affirm
life

push
my expiry date

further
into the future.

Perception

I looked in my car's sideview mirror
and saw how closely

I was being followed

only slowly realizing
I was watching the side of my own car.

September 5, 2014

A hot day
giving a surprise

of thunder
at 8:45 a.m.

like a load of lumber
sliding off a truck

I looked out to see the truck
saw lightning instead

She Would Have Named Them Nubbies

Barbara's skin was itchy during palliative care
due to increasing dosages of morphine
to curtail the pain of abdominal cancer.

I rubbed her skin—arms, abdomen, back, sides, and legs—
every day with a pair of cotton garden gloves.

Little bumps or piles formed on the gloves
made them more effective.

I so wished she would look at the bumps
and tell me they were "nubbies"

but she couldn't see through
the fog of morphine and pain.

I have the gloves, but I don't wear them.

Windy Night

A shadow
of the yew branch

backlit
by a streetlamp

hovers
across

my
window blind

mail
slot
rattles

walls
click

and
creak

Yacht

Yacht
a strange-looking word

a remnant
from a lost language

or
German

(Dutch jacht = hunt)
(German acht = eight)

a strange word
like a hatchet

with a misshapen
handle

Words

Yo't
pronounced yacht

contraction of
you ought

Ivan
Ott

had
a motorboat

not
a yacht

that
cost a lot

no
yo't or yacht

for
Ivan
Ott

yo't—informal companion
to youse

waitress
talk

Under The Bark

For Jackie Morris, saddened at the loss of the beautiful tree

A few years after the blue spruce was cut down
leaving a ten-foot-high stump

a piece of bark
fell off, revealing

thousands of carpenter ants
thick and busy, engraving lines of travel

Privet

Still
hot
air

no breeze
to move

the privet's
leaves

a hidden
flock

of
sparrows

gently, here
and there

jiggle
twigs

In Spring

creeks
and
ditches

flow
like
rivers

On A Hilltop, Near Drumbo

Two
cows

in the sky

except
where hooves and heads

touch
earth

Tamarack

Last
year's

golden
needles

lie
along the roadside

like
rust

Northville Plaza

Midday
on a mild day

the parking lot
half filled

no cars arriving
or leaving

no one
walking

only
a seagull

and two
sparrows

hopping
about

within
a long moment

Strange

to visit this place
that was familiar

when I played among cedars and pines
no taller than I was

now a place
of tall trees

“That was $150 not well spent”

Catherine, I said I wouldn’t write a poem about this
and you replied it might make a good one.

So, here goes. The title is what you said after
telling me that recently you took your youngest

for a session with a psychiatrist
and he hid under a table

the whole time
refusing to speak!

Signs: May

Snagged
on a dead weed

a plastic bag
wavers in the breeze like a flag

tugs
the bending stalk

Rhyme

Imogen
Heap's

voice
leaps

I
weep

A Speeding Squirrel's

oscillating tail
delineates

a near perfect
waveform

Winter Will Come

My vision greyed
as I viewed the landscape.

The car's windows were clean,
and I checked my eyeglasses.

My eyesight
in decline? I wondered.

Then saw the sky
as dull as the land

no bright spot
in the grey overhead blanket.

Ampersand

A long name
for a single character

replacing
a short word held

within
the long name

To Kate Belair

When we met a few months ago
it was a treat to talk

we both had studied at the University of Waterloo
you about 40 years after me

and I noticed
you have a very nice bum

While I headed into the gas station yesterday
I saw a young woman ahead

with a bum like yours, even said to myself
that girl has a bum like Kate's

you paid and then turned
and you were Kate

We chatted for a few minutes
about John Bray Day

May I state, Kate
that you have a very nice bum?

Windy

Take 1

The windy road
around
the placid lake

Take 2

The windy road
around
the rough lake

This Day

Grey
air

not
a metaphor

sky
overcast

blowing
snow

absence
of light

More Than A Fashion Statement

For Sheila Vollmer

I found a faded photo taken when
I was one and a half years old.

I'm wearing sox and shoes.
My tummy sticks out.

Barbara told me for years
I have a baby's tummy.

On seeing the photo
I'm reminded of a young friend

who years ago
came for a visit wearing

a see-through blouse, blue jeans,
and heavy work boots.

When I opened the front door
I said "Nice boots."

She replied "Thanks.
They're Doc Martens."

A King Kong Of A Weed

For William Hawkins, chronicler of King Kong

A King Kong of a weed has arrived in Bruce County
along the banks of Catfish Creek

looks like Queen Anne's lace
but taller, its common names

giant hogweed
giant cow parsley

native to the Caucasus and central Asia
spread in giant leaps into western Europe

imported as an ornamental
to northern United States

into southern Ontario, flourishing
along roadsides and streams

in bush and wasteland,
perennial, living several years

it forms a leafy canopy five feet tall
flowers once in its lifetime

the flower-bearing stems from ten feet tall
up to sixteen feet in *Ontario Weeds*

the juice of this plant brings
skin blisters and blindness

township workers encircle clusters
with rope, cautionary tape, and warning signs

Private Conversations

Early morning
mourning doves converse

speaking slowly
in low tones.

July 3, 2014—Three Performances

For Annis Karpenko

Exploring
ants

run
up

and across
my front steps

*

Chipmunks
high tail it

back and forth
across the parking lot

*

Selah Sue
on YouTube

gives a
high-energy rendition

with
Triggerfinger

of Duffy's
"Mercy"

It's Spring!

People are outdoors
picking up sticks

digging holes
moving dirt

one place
to another.

Chewing Water

Following radiation treatment
on a cancerous vocal cord

my throat narrowed
seemed tight

I chewed water
before I could swallow it

Retinal Retention

Rapidly
passing
birds

draw horizontal lines
across my kitchen window

Barbara Dying

While Barbara was in palliative care
experiencing aphasia and dementia

I wanted her
to remain alive—

her being
in the world

was a comfort
I knew

would
vanish

Spring

Buds
and blossoms

flood
the grey landscape

with
reds

yellows
blues

Whereness

For R. Bruce Elder

A lane
into a farmer's field

goes
nowhere

the field
is there

ploughed
or seeded

it
has

is-
ness

in
transition

Birthdays

Well,
if nothing else

we celebrate
being

not
dead.

A Chipmunk Mystery

It runs
across the parking lot

forth
and back

same
path

all day
every day

—at least
while I watch—

into
shrubbery

at
each end

In My Old Age

Listening to a radio interview
I heard the word "razzle"

several
times

then realized
the word was "arousal"

Fishing

For and after Patricia Moore, and the kids

Pat Moore
taught little kids on Manitoulin Island

where one day
she found them

gathered around the aquarium
at the back of the classroom

fishing for goldfish
with a staple tied to a string

My Friend

I hope you have
a sufficiently

deficient
memory

that you don't recognize
that nearly all I say

I have said to you
in the past

Bucolic

Moving slowly
along a rural road

with the car's
windows
open

on a hot
afternoon

I smell
the roadside dead

Yikes!

I delivered lumber
while I was a teenager

for a house
under construction

that's
now abandoned

Woodlots, Old Cemeteries, Lanes

woodlots
old cemeteries

overgrown
lanes

lanes
to vacant farmhouses

lanes
to crumbling foundations

lanes
to grassy mounds

lanes
to fields of corn stubble

lanes
leading nowhere

Campbell Trail, Ayr, Ontario

Jiggling light
a play of fitful sound

through leaves and trunks
beside the Campbell Trail

tell
a small waterfall

April And May

Incessant
rain

fits
Canada Geese

to
every

flooded
field

mud
puddle

and
ditch

After Major Surgery

I stood at the foot of Barbara's hospital bed
as she wavered into consciousness

opened her eyes, smiled, said "Nelson,
you are covered all over with butterflies

flying out from your elbows."
"Really?" I said. "Yes, they are nice" she replied.

I was overjoyed she was alive—
the butterflies were a bonus.

Notes

Barbara Caruso (1937-2009), my late wife, was brilliant. She was a visual artist (paintings, drawings, prints), poet, essayist, memoirist, and small press publisher (Seripress, presspresspress).

We met in 1964 and married less than five months later, in January 1965. Prior to knowing anything about me, Barbara had read one of my poems in *Volume 63*, liked the sensibility, and wanted to meet me. I had published her drawings in *Volume 63* and I wanted to meet her. I was told she would be staying with her parents in Kincardine prior to returning to the Ontario College of Art (Toronto) in the fall for her final year. My parents' cottage was near Kincardine so it was simple to meet her while I was at the cottage. I immediately wanted to marry her—she was so intelligent, and our interests and what we cared most about coincided. Our lives meshed. I still can't believe my luck in meeting her.

I stopped writing for an extended period in the 1970s and early 1980s. Barbara told me she wanted her poet back, that she had married me because I was a poet. I began writing again in 1987, after we moved from Toronto to Paris. This made her happy. She would be pleased I've continued writing since her death.

My writing helps me cope with my loss. I still consult Barbara, aloud and frequently. She tells me to do things I know I should do but have been avoiding. She remains a vivid and wonderful presence inside my head, an addition to the legacy of her artworks and writings.

"Affiliations And Afflictions"
In this *roman à clef*, we are Catherine Stevenson, Suzan Yates, Stuart Ross, Nelson Ball, Kemeny Babineau, Mary Neff, Jackie Morris.

"After Major Surgery"
This surgery was unrelated to Barbara's final illness.

"After The Visitors Stop Coming"
Hullett Township, a few kilometres north of Clinton, Ontario, in Huron County, is where my paternal ancestors established farms when they emigrated from England in the 1840s. Ball's Church is a small structure located within the cemetery. Ball's Bridge is a two-span iron bridge crossing the Maitland River. It was built in 1885 when an engineer, smitten by one of the Ball girls, persuaded the county to build it. The girls previously crossed on foot through the river when journeying to nearby Goderich. The bridge has been preserved. There is also Ball's Line, a gravelled township road of less than two kilometres' length.

"All And Everything"
This is the overall title of G. I. Gurdjieff's trilogy, the final volume of which is titled *Life Is Real Only Then, When 'I Am'*. Gurdjieff was an influential spiritual teacher who believed that people lived in a state of hypnotic "waking sleep". He taught that people could, through conscious work to develop latent potentialities, achieve greater consciousness. He advocated self-awareness and self-remembering to overcome daydreaming and absentmindedness. The former were habits that Barbara had adopted long before she read Gurdjieff. The clearest discussion of Gurdjieff and his teaching was written by Russian mathematician and philosopher P. D. Ouspensky. I found the writings of Ouspensky more accessible than Gurdjieff's. Gurdjieff influenced numerous modern thinkers and writers, including Carlos Castaneda, Timothy Leary, Alan Watts, and Frank Lloyd Wright. There is a substantial account of Gurdjieff and his teaching on Wikipedia.

"Becky Taylor"
My family did not have TV in 1947, nor did we have access to movies. I was too young to listen to radio drama. Becky's dad's job was a complete mystery to me.

"Campbell Trail, Ayr, Ontario"

The Campbell Trail is a winding walking trail through a large woodlot, a portion of which is wetland, in the central core of the village of Ayr. In length the trail is the equivalent of several street blocks and it connects Watson and Jedburgh Ponds. The forestation is so dense that a walker can't see the ponds or the small connecting creek except at the trail's eastern end where the Jedburgh Dam feeds the creek. At the western end, the outflow from the Watson Dam feeds in to the nearby Nith River.

It is a lovely wilderness walk. Windfall and deadwood are removed only from the path. Lots of snakes, chipmunks, rabbits, and a constant chorus of birds. Trees rub and squeak, a spring gurgles. There is no street noise. It is both a quiet place and quite noisy with nature.

Barbara was a student for several years in her late teens at the Doon Summer School of Fine Art. Class painting expeditions to Ayr were frequent. She saved some of her paintings, including a view of the pump and sink in Mr. Patterson's Hardware and a view of the backs of the Stanley Street businesses seen from the opposite side of Watson Pond.

Barbara had a fondness for Ayr that came to the fore when we moved from Toronto to nearby Paris in 1985. It soon became our favoured destination. There we walked on the streets and on the Campbell Trail and sat beside Watson Pond, watching ducks and swans and eating ice cream.

Following the death of our friend bpNichol, neither of us could focus on work. We came each day for a week to walk the Campbell Trail and sit by one or other of the ponds. A search for needed serenity.

One of Barbara's friends at the Doon school was instructor Jim Gordaneer, slightly older than her. He was Barbara's mentor for a time. They explored the streets of Ayr, observing the architecture of the houses. Occasionally they had lunch at the Queen's Tavern. Barbara somehow managed to get served beer at the Queen's despite being underage. This is ironic in that Barbara was childlike in appearance and remained so through her 30s. When she and I drank at Bassel's Tavern in Toronto, she was always asked to prove her age. Barbara and Jim remained lifelong friends. When Barbara and I explored the streets of Ayr, she recalled architectural detail of houses she had seen many years earlier.

Both ponds were created as millponds. The Jedburgh has an unusual appearance. The dam was built in 1832 and the high water flooded a portion of the white cedar forest that bordered the creek. The pond is populated with tallish, jagged tree stumps. It is a peculiarly haunting sight, enhanced by the apparent stillness of the pond. Only a short portion of the pond's shoreline, including the area of the dam, faces a street. Otherwise it is surrounded by wilderness.

The eastern half of Watson Pond is in wilderness. The western half is in part a public park. These waterways in Ayr are within the Cedar Creek subwatershed, which runs from the nearby village of Roseville to join the Nith River in central Ayr. Large portions of this subwatershed have been designated environmentally sensitive.

"Chewing Water"

This poem is dedicated to Dr. Jim Wright, Radiation Oncologist, Juravinski Cancer Centre, Hamilton, Ontario, to my sister Liz Ball, and to her oncologist friend Dr. Dianne Miller. Dr. Miller talked with Dr. Wright. They persuaded me to try chemo and radiation instead of having my voice box surgically removed. I am enormously grateful.

For several weeks at the end of radiation treatment, I was unable to eat solid food. Swallowing was difficult and it took me an hour to drink one cup of water. I would chew the water, an action that seemed to prepare my throat for the act of swallowing.

"Farmer's Dell Plaza"

This ironically named shopping plaza is located in Brantford at the intersection of two heavily travelled streets and close to an overpass and ramp to Highway 403, a provincial highway.

"July 3, 2014"
Selah Sue is a young Belgian singer/songwriter who writes and performs in English, her second language. Very charming. Triggerfinger is a Belgian rock band. The energetic performance referred to was filmed at the 2010 Lowlands Festival in the Netherlands. Annis and I are Selah Sue fans!

"A King Kong Of A Weed"
William Hawkins wrote a series of King Kong poems in the 1960s. Their titles include "King Kong Goes to Rotterdam", "King Kong Meets Allen Ginsberg", and "King Kong Goes to Saudi-Arabia". They are rambunctious, reflective, and reappear in *The Collected Poems of William Hawkins* (Chaudiere Books, 2015).

Ontario Weeds is Publication 505 from the Ontario Ministry of Agriculture and Food, 1992.

"Lake Huron Shoreline, Revised"
The shoreline revealed in this poem is located near the family cottage (a humble log cabin constructed for my mother, her mother, and a girlfriend of my mother, in 1939; the lot and logs cost $25) on the bay at the foot of the 8th Concession of Bruce Township, Bruce County, a few kilometres north of the village of Inverhuron. The cottage, complete with resident bats and mice, now belongs to my sister Liz and me. The water level seen in this poem was extremely low. In 2015, the levels were high, the highest they had been in years. I made the observations in the poem on a visit there on a mild day in March 2012. The high water level in 2015 was reported by Liz after she stayed there in June.

"Local Wildlife"
A rather thin coyote ate crabapples on the front lawn of a townhouse across the street from my home for three days in a row. A three-day bender? It had no sense of vehicular traffic and for prolonged periods stopped the cars in both directions while it mean-

dered on the street. This is an uncommon diet for a coyote. They usually eat animals, ranging from insects to deer and, frequently, domesticated dogs.

There is an excess of poetic licence in this poem. Black bears have been spotted in at least Bruce, Huron, and Oxford counties. They are common in the Georgian Bay area, as are rattlesnakes. Massasauga rattlesnakes are found as far south in Ontario as the north shore of Lake Erie in the Wainfleet Bog near Port Colborne. Sightings of grey wolves occur in southwestern Ontario. The bears are shy of humans; the rattlesnakes are unperturbed until stepped on. Grey wolves may be a problem for farmers, but they are less common than coyotes. Cross-breeding occurs among wolves, dogs, and coyotes.

"More Than A Fashion Statement"

Sheila told me recently it was not her intention to wear a see-through blouse. The transparency was the consequence of the thinness of the material of the blouse and the intense sunlight at our front door. Our front door, made of stainless steel and plate glass, receives many hours of direct sunlight in the summer. This causes a different kind of problem as well: the doorsill, also steel, will expand in the heat and jam the door so that it won't open. We use the side door during these times. It is shaded and made of wood.

"My Friend Catherine"

Catherine Stevenson studied history and fine art with an emphasis on photography at York University and then studied education. She teaches enrichment classes for smart kids in the Waterloo Region District School Board. She taught children's classes at the Royal Ontario Museum in Toronto for ten years. She has begun designing and teaching academic programs for children in the Summer Enrichment Day Camps at Wilfrid Laurier University in Waterloo. These camps have the overall name LEAP (Laurier Enriched Academic Program), and the symbol is a picture of a leaping frog. I've long thought the resemblance between very young children and frogs is remarkable.

Catherine was for five years the Museum Curator at the Adelaide Hunter Hoodless Homestead National Historic Site located near St. George, Ontario. She shares with her partner Clayton Barker a passion for museum work and things antiquarian. Her priority is the development and education of her two young boys. Catherine takes finely composed still photographs in addition to creating videos. She also gathers very small pieces of driftwood that she makes into aesthetically interesting nestlike arrangements that lurk within her home in Waterford, ready to surprise the observant explorer.

I met Catherine by happy coincidence on the grounds of the Homestead in October 2011—she was outdoors in the open-air picnic shelter working on a course assignment while I was walking the grounds for exercise and distraction. We began a conversation that remains ongoing.

Catherine was intrigued by the building I occupy in Paris and how Barbara and I used its spaces. She decided to record this. Her project lasted 14 months and was completed in November 2014. The 35-minute video is titled *Nelson Ball & Barbara Caruso / Home Project / A Photo Documentary*.

The first public screening of the video occurred at the Homestead during the 2014 Mansfield Press Fall Book Launch, which included my *Some Mornings*. It was a wonderful event, well-attended, hosted by Catherine and her son Lucas for the video, Stuart Ross and Denis De Klerck for the books, and quietly but effectively by Jackie Shute and Kate Belair, and silently by the absent Joanna Rickert-Hall, for the Homestead. Readings from the books were given by the authors Frank Davey, Laura Farina, Christine Miscione, and guest Brian David Johnston reading my poems. Catherine's video can be seen on YouTube.

Hamilton Arts & Letters online magazine is also hosting Catherine's video, with a foreword by Stephen Broomer and an afterword by Judith Sandiford.

Catherine gave the following e-mail interview about the video to arts journalist Colleen Toms as background for an article Colleen wrote for *Brant News.*

CT: *Why did you do the documentary on Nelson and Barbara?*
CS: Nelson probably mentioned that, until recently, I was the Curator of the Adelaide Hunter Hoodless Homestead. When Nelson took me on a tour of his home, I was struck by the fact that the second floor (which was Barbara's studio floor) seemed to have been frozen in time. As if Barbara had just stepped out for a moment. I also knew that both Barbara and Nelson are noted figures in recent Canadian art and literature.

The idea for the video came during a discussion with my partner Clayton Barker, who also has extensive experience in museums. We thought that the space should be recorded because it was important (for the reasons outlined above).

At first, I tried to record it as a curator would record a space—in a very objective, linear and thorough manner. As time went on, I took some small artistic liberties: I left some rooms out and dabbled with giving a "sense" of the place.

In its final form, I am happy with the fact that my presence as "filmmaker" is very lightly felt and that the emphasis is on the space and a residual sense of the people who live(d) there.

CT: *How long have you known him and how did you meet?*
CS: Nelson will probably be better able to tell you, but I think we met in the fall of 2011. It was on a Sunday, and it was a beautiful autumn day. I was in the Homestead's picnic shelter, working on an assignment and watching for visitors. Nelson was out on a walk. We started chatting, and hit it off right away. We never really stopped chatting since then.

CT: What are you hoping will come from the documentary?

CS: I was mostly hoping that I would finish it. Which I did. (Yay!) I was also hoping that both Nelson and I would be happy with it. Which we are. Beyond that, everything I was hoping for has already happened. Now it has a life of its own.

CT: What do you think of Nelson as a poet and individual?

CS: I am far from an expert on poetry. I always feel completely unqualified to answer any questions about Nelson's work. However, I can say that (as a reader of his work) his style of writing speaks so clearly, purely, and meaningfully, about the essence of things. About details and feelings that can too easily be ignored. I am truly a fan of his work.

Regarding Nelson as an individual—he has enriched my life so wonderfully. I enjoy hearing his insights and perspective on topics. I enjoy the peacefulness that I experience when I have conversations with him. I enjoy hearing about his world. He is a lovely person.

I am deeply grateful to Catherine for her friendship. She and her boys inspire me. Her friendship has enabled me to confront my loss of Barbara, to find equilibrium. I hope our ongoing conversation is as rewarding for Catherine as it is for me.

"Orderliness"

Our mother was a Mossop. Her paternal grandfather, Thomas (1830–1875), a ship's captain and marine engineer, came from Ireland in the 1850s to dredge the harbour at Bayfield for a grain company. While Mossop worked on this task, jurisdiction for the harbour transferred from the grain company to the government and neither paid him for his work. He farmed for a while. In the 1860s, he owned and operated Mossop's Commercial Hotel. It later became the attractive and well-known Little Inn in Bayfield.

"September 5, 2014"
Regulations regarding road safety were less stringent in the 1950s, when I was young. It wasn't too unusual for a delivery of lumber to slide off the end of a truck and spill onto the roadway. Some loads were more thoroughly secured than others.

"To Kate Belair"
The amazing whirlwind that is Kate was the Volunteer Development Coordinator for the Adelaide Hunter Hoodless Homestead Museum. Later, she became Executive Director of the Federated Women's Institutes of Canada. She re-envisioned the role of the Branch WIs to focus on charity fundraising in ways that will bring an influx of younger women into the organization. Her office was located at the Homestead.

Adelaide Hoodless (1858–1910) was an impassioned promoter of a better and safer life for rural women and children through her many efforts, including co-founding the Women's Institutes.

John Bray was a veteran of the War of 1812 who settled here, built the first farmhouse, and lived here until 1852, when the property was sold to David Hunter, Adelaide's father. Bray was celebrated at an event in 2013, curated by Catherine Stevenson.

"Yikes!"
I worked only two summers for Ball-Macaulay Limited, my father's builders' supplies business in Seaforth, Ontario. The manual labour required was too difficult for my tall and skinny physique.

Acknowledgements

Thanks to readers of drafts of the poems, including Cameron Anstee, Kemeny Babineau, Liz Ball, Clayton Barker, Kate Belair, Anita Campbell, Patrick Campbell, Larry Cowan, Brian David Johnston, Dave Little, Trisha Little, James McDonald, Patricia Moore, Jackie Morris, Mary Neff, Stuart Ross, Heather Smith, and Catherine Stevenson. I'm grateful for your support and suggestions.

Special thanks to Stuart Ross, who spotted in my poems weaknesses that had eluded me. A mutual friend and editor once commented to me that Stuart is perhaps the best poetry editor in Canada.

I'm grateful to Cameron Anstee, Patrick Campbell, Annis Karpenko, and James McDonald, who endorsed lengthy endnotes when I was uncertain about them.

Jill Yuzwa kick-started my research on the ponds at Ayr by commenting that the creek in my poem may be named Cedar Creek. The geographical and historical information in my note on the Campbell Trail comes from a report prepared by Green Scheels Pidgeon Planning Consultants titled "Township of North Dumfries, Ayr Community Plan, Final Report, July 2003". Elsewhere, I found a single reference to Watson Creek, but the creek bearing that name, which may be an informal name, was not given a location.

Some of these poems appeared in the chapbooks *All And Everything* (Laurel Reed Books), *Small Waterways* (Apt. 9 Press), *Thirty Poems* (my Rubblestone Press), and *This Close To Being A Tree* (Monk Press). Thanks to the editors Kemeny Babineau, Cameron Anstee, and Larry Cowan.

Some of the poems appeared previously in the online magazine *Hamilton Arts & Letters* (8:2), the websites *The Week Shall Inherit The Verse* (June 22, 2015), *One Sentence Poems* (October 22, 2015), and *Dusie: Tuesday Poem* (February 16, 2016), edited respectively by Paul Lisson and Fiona Kinsella, Stuart Ross, Dale Wisely and Robert Scotellaro, and rob mclennan. Poems also appeared in a typewritten booklet issued by Jim Clinefelter's press-press-pull/alabastine press in Portland, Oregon, in leaflets issued by my Rubblestone Press, and in the poetry magazines *Illiterature, Industrial Sabotage,* and *Stone The Crows!* edited by Michael e. Casteels, jwcurry, and Larry Cowan. Two of the poems appeared in the *Windsor Review* (Fall 2014), in a special issue titled *Alice Munro: A Souwesto Celebration,* guest-edited by Tim Struthers and John B. Lee for managing editor Marty Gervais.

Thanks to Catherine Stevenson and Colleen Toms for permission to use the interview appended to my note on the poem "My Friend Catherine". Colleen's article, titled "A prolific and poetic two years for Nelson Ball", is about my book *Some Mornings* and Catherine's video *Nelson Ball & Barbara Caruso / Home Project / A Photo Documentary*. The article was published in the January 8, 2015, issue of *Brant News*.

Thank you, Stuart, for choosing these poems for "a stuart ross book", and thank you, Denis, for the cover design and for publishing this book. I'm grateful to both of you.

These poems were written from 2013 to 2015. Thanks to the Ontario Arts Council for Writers' Reserve grants that enabled my writing in 2014.

Nelson Ball
March 2016

Nelson Ball is a poet and bookseller living in Paris, Ontario. He has worked as a labourer, chauffeur, clerk, seasonal forest ranger, record store clerk, and janitor. From 1965 to 1973 he ran the legendary Weed/Flower Press, publishing mimeo editions of early books by Victor Coleman, Carol Bergé, David McFadden, bill bissett, bpNichol, and many others. He is the author of more than 40 poetry books and chapbooks.

Other Books From Mansfield Press

Poetry

Leanne Averbach, *Fever*
Tara Azzopardi, *Last Stop, Lonesome Town*
Nelson Ball, *In This Thin Rain*
Nelson Ball, *Some Mornings*
Gary Barwin, *Moon Baboon Canoe*
George Bowering, *Teeth: Poems 2006–2011*
Stephen Brockwell, *Complete Surprising Fragments of Improbable Books*
Stephen Brockwell & Stuart Ross, eds., *Rogue Stimulus: The Stephen Harper Holiday Anthology for a Prorogued Parliament*
Diana Fitzgerald Bryden, *Learning Russian*
Alice Burdick, *Book of Short Sentences*
Alice Burdick, *Flutter*
Alice Burdick, *Holler*
Sarah Burgoyne, *Saint Twin*
Jason Camlot, *What The World Said*
Margaret Christakos, *wipe.under.a.love*
Pino Coluccio, *First Comes Love*
Marie-Ève Comtois, *My Planet of Kites*
Dani Couture, *YAW*
Gary Michael Dault, *The Milk of Birds*
Frank Davey, *Poems Suitable to Current Material Conditions*
Pier Giorgio Di Cicco, *The Dark Time of Angels*
Pier Giorgio Di Cicco, *Dead Men of the Fifties*
Pier Giorgio Di Cicco, *The Honeymoon Wilderness*
Pier Giorgio Di Cicco, *Living in Paradise*
Pier Giorgio Di Cicco, *Early Works*
Pier Giorgio Di Cicco, *The Visible World*
Salvatore Difalco, *What Happens at Canals*
Christopher Doda, *Aesthetics Lesson*
Christopher Doda, *Among Ruins*
Glen Downie, *Monkey Soap*
Rishma Dunlop, *The Body of My Garden*
Rishma Dunlop, *Lover Through Departure: New and Selected Poems*
Rishma Dunlop, *Metropolis*
Rishma Dunlop & Priscila Uppal, eds., *Red Silk: An Anthology of South Asian Women Poets*
Ollivier Dyens, *The Profane Earth*
Laura Farina, *Some Talk of Being Human*
Jaime Forsythe, *Sympathy Loophole*
Carole Glasser Langille, *Late in a Slow Time*
Eva HD, *Rotten Perfect Mouth*
Eva HD, *Wolverine States*
Suzanne Hancock, *Another Name for Bridge*
Jason Heroux, *Emergency Hallelujah*
Jason Heroux, *Hard Work Cheering Up Sad Machines*
Jason Heroux, *Memoirs of an Alias*
Jason Heroux, *Natural Capital*
John B. Lee, *In the Terrible Weather of Guns*
Jeanette Lynes, *The Aging Cheerleader's Alphabet*
David W. McFadden, *Abnormal Brain Sonnets*
David W. McFadden, *Be Calm, Honey*
David W. McFadden, *Shouting Your Name Down the Well: Tankas and Haiku*
David W. McFadden, *What's the Score?*
Kathryn Mockler, *The Purpose Pitch*
Leigh Nash, *Goodbye, Ukulele*
Lillian Necakov, *The Bone Broker*
Lillian Necakov, *Hooligans*
Peter Norman, *At the Gates of the Theme Park*
Peter Norman, *Water Damage*
Natasha Nuhanovic, *Stray Dog Embassy*
Catherine Owen & Joe Rosenblatt, *Dog*
Corrado Paina, *The Alphabet of the Traveler*
Corrado Paina, *Cinematic Taxi*
Corrado Paina, *The Dowry of Education*
Corrado Paina, *Hoarse Legend*
Corrado Paina, *Souls in Plain Clothes*
Nick Papaxanthos, *Love Me Tender*
Stuart Ross et al., *Our Days in Vaudeville*
Matt Santateresa, *A Beggar's Loom*
Matt Santateresa, *Icarus Redux*
Ann Shin, *The Last Thing Standing*
Jim Smith, *Back Off, Assassin! New and Selected Poems*
Jim Smith, *Happy Birthday, Nicanor Parra*
Robert Earl Stewart, *Campfire Radio Rhapsody*
Robert Earl Stewart, *Something Burned on the Southern Border*
Carey Toane, *The Crystal Palace*
Aaron Tucker, *Punchlines*
Priscila Uppal, *Sabotage*
Priscila Uppal, *Summer Sport: Poems*
Priscila Uppal, *Winter Sport: Poems*
Steve Venright, *Floors of Enduring Beauty*
Brian Wickers, *Stations of the Lost*

Fiction

Marianne Apostolides, *The Lucky Child*
Sarah Dearing, *The Art of Sufficient Conclusions*
Denis De Klerck, ed., *Particle & Wave: A Mansfield Omnibus of Electro-Magnetic Fiction*
Salvatore Difalco, *Mean Season*
Paula Eisenstein, *Flip Turn*
Sara Heinonen, *Dear Leaves, I Miss You All*
Christine Miscione, *Carafola*
Marko Sijan, *Mongrel*
Tom Walmsley, *Dog Eat Rat*
Corinne Wasilewski, *Live from the Underground*

Non-Fiction

George Bowering, *How I Wrote Certain of My Books*
Denis De Klerck & Corrado Paina, eds., *College Street–Little Italy: Toronto's Renaissance Strip*
Pier Giorgio Di Cicco, *Municipal Mind: Manifestos for the Creative City*
Amy Lavender Harris, *Imagining Toronto*
David W. McFadden, *Mother Died Last Summer*
Deborah Verginella, ed., *Buon Appetito Toronto!*

For a complete list of Mansfield Press titles, please visit mansfieldpress.net